Our Amazing States™

Alaska
The Last Frontier

Marcia Amidon Lusted

PowerKiDS press™

New York

Published in 2011 by The Rosen Publishing Group, Inc.
29 East 21st Street, New York, NY 10010

First Edition

Editor: Maggie Murphy
Book Design: Greg Tucker
Photo Researcher: Jessica Gerweck

Photo Credits: Cover, pp. 5, 9, 13, 19, 22 (tree, flag, flower) Shutterstock.com; p. 7 Hulton Archive/ Getty Images; p. 11 Burgess Blevins/Getty Images; p. 15 © Alaska Stock/age fotostock; p. 17 David Job/Getty Images; p. 22 (fish) www.iStockphoto.com/lightasafeather; p. 22 (bird) www.iStockphoto. com/Suzann Julien; p. 22 (Curt Schilling) J. Meric/Getty Images; p. 22 (Irene Bedard) Donato Sardella/ WireImage/Getty Images; p. 22 (Mario Chalmers) Robert Laberge/Getty Images.

Library of Congress Cataloging-in-Publication Data

Lusted, Marcia Amidon.
  Alaska : the last frontier / Marcia Amidon Lusted. — 1st ed.
     p. cm. — (Our amazing states)
  Includes index.
  ISBN 978-1-4488-0666-9 (library binding) — ISBN 978-1-4488-0769-7 (pbk.) — ISBN 978-1-4488-0770-3 (6-pack)
  1. Alaska—Juvenile literature. I. Title.
  F904.3.L87 2011
  979.8—dc22
                                         2010004666

Manufactured in the United States of America

CPSIA Compliance Information: Batch #WS10PK: For Further Information contact Rosen Publishing, New York, New York at 1-800-237-9932

Contents

The Last Frontier

This state is made up of a large piece of land and many smaller islands. It is called the Last Frontier because there are large areas of wilderness there. You can find **tundra**, volcanoes, and even rain forests there. Where are you? You are in Alaska!

Alaska is located on the west coast of North America. Alaska is north of Washington but does not share a border with any other state. Instead, Alaska shares a border only with Canada. To the west is the Gulf of Alaska and the Bering Sea. Across the Bering Sea is Russia.

In Alaska, colorful lights sometimes fill the night sky. People often use airplanes to get places instead of driving cars. These things and more make Alaska a special state.

Here, you can see the northern lights, or aurora borealis, in the sky over Copper City, Alaska. These lights can be seen from many places in the state.

Explorers and Gold Seekers

About 15,000 years ago, early humans crossed a land bridge from present-day Russia into what is now western Alaska. Over many years, people slowly **migrated** from Alaska to other parts of North America. However, some people stayed in Alaska.

In the eighteenth century, **explorers** sailed from Russia to Alaska. They found native peoples living there, as well as many fur seals and otters. The explorers built trading posts for selling furs. In 1867, the United States bought Alaska from the Russian Empire for $7 million.

In 1880, gold was discovered in Alaska. Many people came to look for gold. People and supplies were carried by dogsled over snowy trails. In 1959, Alaska became the forty-ninth state.

This picture shows a group of gold miners in Klondike, Alaska, in 1897. After gold was found in Alaska, towns and cities were built quickly for the miners and gold-related businesses there.

A Place of Extremes

Alaska is by far the largest state in the United States. Most of the state is surrounded by bodies of water, such as the Gulf of Alaska, the Bering Sea, the Pacific Ocean, and the Arctic Ocean.

Northern Alaska is flat and treeless, but the middle of the state has mountain ranges. There, North America's highest mountain, Mount McKinley, rises 20,320 feet (6,194 m) above the ground. Southwest Alaska has many active volcanoes. You can find large masses of ice called **glaciers** in southeast Alaska, as well as many trees. The state also has millions of lakes and rivers, including the Yukon River.

Alaska has several different **climates**. Southern Alaska's forests are warm and wet, while northern Alaska has long, dark winters.

Mount McKinley, shown here, is sometimes called Mount Denali. The word *denali* comes from the language of Alaska's Athabaskan people and means "the high one."

Alaska's Native Peoples

Many of the people who live in Alaska are from **indigenous** cultures. The Inupiats, the Yupiks, and the Aleuts are among Alaska's many native peoples.

The Yupik and Inupiat peoples are sometimes known as Eskimos. Today, many Inupiat and Yupik people live in modern houses in small towns all around the state. The Aleut people are from Alaska's Aleutian Islands. They once traveled long distances in small sea **kayaks**, hunting for seals and whales. Other native peoples, such as the Tlingits and Haidas, live in Alaska's southeast coastal areas.

Some native Alaskan peoples still rely on the land for food. They hunt, fish, and gather berries and other foods. Alaska has passed a law protecting land that the native peoples need to survive.

These children are Alaskan Inupiats. Many Inupiats live in Barrow, Alaska, which is the northernmost city in Alaska as well as the entire United States.

Watching for Whales and Bears

There is more wildlife than there are people in Alaska. There, you can go whale watching and see humpback, beluga, and blue whales. Bearded seals, walruses, and sea otters swim in Alaska's ocean waters, and salmon swim in its rivers. Caribou, moose, and wolves wander on land. Eagles and owls fly through the skies. The arctic fox changes its coat to match the seasons. Watch out for polar, grizzly, and black bears!

Alaska's forests are filled with birch, spruce, cedar, and hemlock trees. Wild asters, violets, and lupines bloom during the summer. Many wild berries grow in Alaska, such as lingonberries, blueberries, and even nagoonberries.

Here, a brown bear catches a salmon from a waterfall at the Kodiak National Wildlife Refuge, in Kodiak, Alaska.

What Do People Do in Alaska?

Commercial fishing is one of Alaska's biggest **industries**. Chances are that the salmon, shrimp, or Pacific cod on your dinner table were caught in Alaska's waters. Factories in Alaska also freeze and can fish to be sold throughout the world.

In 1968, oil and natural gas were discovered in Alaska. Today oil is transported to other states through the Trans-Alaska Pipeline. The oil industry is the state's most **valuable** industry. Some ranches in Alaska raise reindeer, beef cattle, and horses. Loggers cut trees and sell them to places like Japan.

Many people like to visit Alaska for its beautiful scenery. Some Alaskans work in jobs that provide food, shelter, and entertainment for these visitors.

These commercial fishermen are raising a net full of salmon onto their boat in the Chatham Strait, in southeastern Alaska.

Let's Visit Juneau

The city of Juneau started out as the location of one of Alaska's first big gold discoveries. Today it is the state capital. It is also the only state capital in the country that has no roads leading to it! Visitors to Juneau must fly or take a ferry there.

In Juneau you can visit the Alaska State Museum and see a **totem pole** carved with President Abraham Lincoln's face. You can also ride on the Mount Roberts tramway for a great view of Juneau and the surrounding area.

Visitors to Juneau might want to visit the nearby Mendenhall Glacier or take an airplane tour to see **icebergs**. They can also go on a whale watch and see humpback whales and orcas up close.

Mendenhall Glacier, in Alaska's Mendenhall Valley, is about 12 miles (19 km) long. Ice climbing, shown here, is a popular activity there.

Fjords and Wildlife

Alaska's two national parks are great places to visit. Kenai **Fjords** National Park is home to glaciers, ice fields, and fjords, which are deep sea inlets cut by the movement of glaciers. Visitors to the park can see the glaciers up close and tour the fjords by boat.

Denali National Park, which surrounds Mount McKinley, was the first national park created just to help keep wildlife safe. Here you can see grizzly bears, caribou, and wolves. You can also visit the kennels where the park's sled dogs live. In the winter, these dogs pull sleds through the park for patrols and to help park rangers and researchers travel.

Sea otters, sea lions, seals, and whales are among the many animals that live in the water surrounding Kenai Fjords National Park, shown here.

Come to Alaska!

If you love the outdoors and wildlife, Alaska is a great place to visit. You can watch the Iditarod sled dog race from Anchorage to Nome, which takes place every year in March. At the Valley of Ten Thousand Smokes, in the Aleutian Islands, you can see evidence of one of the biggest volcanic **eruptions** in history.

You can go outside on a spring or fall night and watch the aurora borealis, or northern lights, as they ripple and move through the sky in shifting colors of red, green, and purple. The colors are formed by solar winds in the atmosphere.

Alaska has many beautiful places to see and fun things to do. Take a trip there and see it for yourself!

Glossary

climates (KLY-mits) The kinds of weather certain areas have.

commercial (kuh-MER-shul) Having to do with business or trade.

eruptions (ih-RUP-shunz) Explosions of gases, smoke, or lava from a volcano.

explorers (ek-SPLOR-erz) People who travel and look for new land.

fjords (fee-YORDZ) Deep sea inlets cut by the movement of glaciers.

glaciers (GLAY-shurz) Large masses of ice that move down a mountain or along a valley.

icebergs (YS-burgz) Very large pieces of ice floating in the water.

indigenous (in-DIH-jeh-nus) Having started in and coming naturally from a certain area.

industries (IN-dus-treez) Businesses in which many people work and make money producing a product.

kayaks (KY-aks) Small, light boats that people paddle.

migrated (MY-grayt-ed) Moved from one place to another.

totem pole (TOH-tem POHL) A large pole that is carved or painted with different images.

tundra (TUN-druh) A frozen area with no trees and with black soil.

valuable (VAL-yoo-bul) Important, or worth a lot of money.

Alaska State Symbols

State Tree
Sitka Spruce

State Fish
King Salmon

State Flag

State Bird
Willow
Ptarmigan

State Flower
Forget-Me-Not

State Seal

Famous People from Alaska

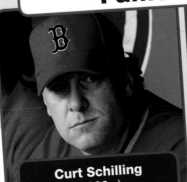
Curt Schilling
(1966–)
Born in Anchorage, AK
Baseball Player

Irene Bedard
(1967–)
Born in Anchorage, AK
Actress/Voice of
Disney's *Pocahontas*

Mario Chalmers
(1986–)
Born in Anchorage, AK
Basketball Player

Alaska State Map

Arctic Ocean

Brooks Range

Bering Strait

Porcupine River

Yukon River

Nome

Fairbanks

Kuskowin River

Alaska Range

Anchorage

Kenai

Seward

Aleutian Range

Juneau

Sitka

Kodiak

Pacific Ocean

Legend

O Major City

⭐ Capital

〜 River

Alaska State Facts

Population: About 626,932

Area: 663,267 square miles (1,717,854 sq km)

Motto: "North to the Future"

Song: "Alaska's Flag," words by Marie Drake and music
by Elinor Dusenbury

23

Index

Web Sites

Due to the changing nature of Internet links, PowerKids Press has developed an online list of Web sites related to the subject of this book. This site is updated regularly. Please use this link to access the list:

www.powerkidslinks.com/amst/ak/